"As the Soul Teaches"

Bill Peter

Beaver's Pond Press
Edina, Minnesota

Dedication

This book on the search for God's will in our lives is dedicated to my mom and dad. As a child, I learned about right and wrong from them. As I grew, I learned about ethics and morality from experiencing life and listening to the teachings of my soul. Although mom and dad have been in the presence of God's eternal love in heaven for years, their moral guidance frequently rushes through my dreams and my conscious mind as I make decisions. God's will for my life may not always be exactly what my parents taught me, but thanks be to God, the messages are extremely complementary.

I'm convinced that mom, dad and God are pleased with my search and my sharing with you, the reader. In that confidence, I find Peace-of-Mind, which I trust will be yours also as you read and reflect on As the Soul Teaches.

About the Cover

Our soul teaches us as if the brightest rays of golden sunlight are breaking through the darkness in our life. God has provided us with an inner divine spirit or soul to guide our behavior throughout our life.

A window to our soul is captured as a frame on the cover, and the theme of windows to the soul is utilized throughout the book.

As the Soul Teaches

The back cover contains slots for a business card so that As the Soul Teaches, given as a gift, is an Enhanced Business Card™. This is the design of all books in the Peace-of-Mind series.

Artist's Statement

As I read the manuscript of As the Soul Teaches, I was struck by its scope. At once huge and intimate in scale, the act of listening to one's soul does not easily lend itself to visual interpretation. In drawing thumbnails, a simple metaphor for introspection emerged: the image of a window. Recurring in all the illustrations in one form or another and mirrored by the way that each illustration panel becomes a window to the viewer, windows became a way to express realization and clarity. In each illustration, some element of the scene in the panel protrudes through the perimeter, one reality infiltrating another.

These are quiet and small drawings that deal with large and important issues. These are sober and calm reflections of our need for self-assessment and awareness in a world full of pressures.

Drawing became a meditative act. In spending time with these still and pensive subjects, I found myself caught up in their reflectiveness.

Ivy Brassil

billpeter.com

Thanks To My Supporters

As the Soul Teaches began as a few poems and grew with the encouragement of a number of people.

Special thanks to Ryan Soderstrom, Daniel Verdick and Milton Adams for their constructive critique on the design, production and marketing of the book. Ivy Brassil provided unique artistic insight as she developed the inspired illustrations that are a very important part of the total message of the book.

Also, very useful suggestions were made by Virginia Matzinger, Jerry Hoganson, Larry Thornton, Kenneth Heiser, Linda Schneider and my wife Arlene Joern-Peter as the book went through its development stages.

Thanks to all for your encouragement and support.

Table of Contents

	Page
Our Blessings	
Overview	13
The Miracle of Creation	15
The Soul's Message	17
Where is God?	19
Heaven and Hell	21
Miracles and Mysteries	23
Where Love Resides	25
The Simple Truth	27
Our Dialog	
Pause and Reflect	29
Body and Soul	33
Observing Ourselves	37
Tears of Sadness and Joy	39
Legal, Amoral and Moral Behavior	43
War and Peace	47
Tapping the Unconscious	
Dreaming	49
The Dreams of Your Life	51
Every Dream Has a Meaning	55
Musings of a Runner	57
And Then, I Prayed	61
Re-Parenting Ourselves	63
Our Emotions	67

bill peter.com

Life's Guideposts

The Flow of Life	69
The Real Facts of Life	73
"Family" Rather Than "Foreigner"	75
Leadership	77
Integrity	79
The Truth, the Whole Truth, and Nothing but the Truth	81
The Moral Compass	83
Let's Play	85
Creative Living	87

Our Behavior

Finding Your Calling	89
A Person's Mindset	93
A Potential Giant Step Toward Tolerance	97
Born Free-Vote to Stay Free	101
Freedom and Responsibility	103
A Shared Vision	105
Reflections on Work	107
Ethics in Business	109
About Work and Society	115

Life in Perspective

Thinking About Thinking	119
Time	123
We Are Our Perception of Ourselves	125
Forgiveness	129

The Power of the Hug 131
A Successful Life 133
We Make the Choices 135
Peace-of-Mind 137

Appendix

About the Author 141
Order Form for As The Soul Teaches 143

OUR BLESSINGS

We have many blessings from God to be thankful for. Our soul, our spiritual essence, is our greatest blessing.

How can we reach our soul?
How can we hear its messages?
How can we see its glory?
How can we experience its guidance?
How can we feel its wisdom?

We see our soul as if through a window. Four windows to our soul are through prayer, meditation, life's experiences and our dreams.

God is seeking to guide us through our soul and we need to focus our attention on God to experience our essence.

Consider windows to the soul:

The window of prayer - a period of contemplation and communication with the divine essence that is within us. How fortunate we are that God has given us a counselor within us that is in perfect harmony with God's will for our lives.

The window of meditation - as we focus on our most important spiritual decisions, we have the wonderful gift of the ability to let go of the messages of the world and to meditate on the important teachings of our soul.

The window of life's experiences - joyful, sad, positive, negative, encouraging, threatening; as we ponder on our unique experiences, we have the ability to determine the lessons we are learning to guide our course on the path of unconditional love and compassion for our Peace-of-Mind.

The window of our dreams - what a treasure of the deepest thoughts from our unconscious mind; lessons from our joys and our fears that we can analyze to enrich our understanding of God's will for our lives.

Windows have two sides. How exciting it is that our soul is constantly seeking us even as we are seeking the teachings of our soul through the four windows of prayer, meditation, life's experiences and our dreams.

Windows to the soul; we just have to use them to enjoy a full, rich life and Peace-of-Mind.

Overview

As the Soul Teaches…we learn about the essence of being human.

This book is designed as an opportunity to pause and reflect on the teachings from our souls. It is not a book about any particular religion, but it is about our basic spiritual nature as human beings.

Sometimes the teachings from our soul reinforce our personal inclinations and sometimes the teachings provide new insights that cause us to review and change our thinking and behavior.

Peace-of-Mind is ours in our everyday living when we listen to and act on the lessons from our souls, our very essence.

As the soul teaches, sometimes we rebel and don't follow its guidance. That we have such free will is a gift from the Creator.

The lessons from our souls are precious, and as we grow to follow them, Peace-of-Mind will be a gift for our lives.

As the Soul Teaches

For our life, for the wonder of our world and for our loving relationships, we thank the Creator.

The Miracle of Creation

We didn't create ourselves; that's obvious. We could not have influenced the egg and sperm that formed us in any way. Therefore, we are here because some force outside us created us.

And our mother and father had no knowledge of how to build a brain, a heart, an eye or a leg. Our parents were part of our creation, but they could not ever be considered the powerful creative force behind our birth.

The creative force behind our birth, the Creator, is miraculous in every way. And that Creator is the same creative force behind the birth of every child, everywhere. The miracle of creation is the Creator. For centuries people have wrestled with the puzzling phenomenon of how creation occurs. Neither scientist nor philosopher has developed any concept that challenges the fact that there is a universal Creator.

The air we breathe, the trees that grow, the soil that is capable of growing food, the sun that keeps us warm, the rain that nourishes the soil, the water that is available for us to drink, the animals, the birds, the stars, the moon, the rivers, the ocean, the mountains and the valleys—all are from the Creator, the miracle of creation.

To think of creation is to be humble. To acknowledge that we are far from the center of the universe and only a small part of it is humbling. We have so much to be thankful for, and it starts with our very existence.

Each day as we awake, we have good reason to be thankful to the Creator for our life, for the wonders of our world and for our family and friends.

As we love and are loved, we recognize that we were created to be in relationship with others. When the relationship turns to hate rather than love, we are painfully aware that something is wrong.

But then, we come to a turning point! The Creator has given us the capacity to both love and hate and the free will to choose. The Creator has empowered us to make the choices between love and hate in every situation and every relationship. The decisions are up to us.

War, violence and anger all come from the emotion of hate. Peace, comfort and nurturing all come from the emotion of love. We get to choose between love and hate literally thousands of times. When we choose love, we are on the path to Peace-of-Mind.

The Creator has given us a free will to make choices. Our lives will be joyous or sad, peaceful or tumultuous, serene or anxious as the result of our choices. That's part of the miracle of creation.

The Soul's Message

Imagine a God who created everything and everyone in the universe and loves everything and everyone.

God loves you and God loves me.

And God has created us in the image of God, so we are all blessed with divinity within our souls.

God blessed us by providing us with a comforter and guide who dwells within us and is available any time we choose to tune into our soul.

If God loves you and is within you and God loves me and is within me, I am encouraged to love you.

The soul's message is clear—tune into the divinity that is within you and love everyone and everything with the unconditional love that God has given to all of us.

Praise God and Praise the Soul's Message That We May Stay True to Our Divinity.

Where is God?

If we are made in the image of God and God loves us all, and if God is within you and within me, then I am encouraged to love you. War, violence, anger and hate can only occur if we decide not to love each other.

Is God somewhere "out there" or is God within each of us? The nature of God, unconditional love as we expect from a heavenly experience, is within each of us. However, with our free will, we can tune into that wellspring of love or reject it. Free will is also a gift from God.

God is present everywhere and can't be restricted to a place, even if we call the place heaven. We can find God through our everyday experiences and through prayer, meditation and dreams. We can search for God's purpose for our lives as we search for love, Peace-of-Mind and the heavenly experience.

As the Soul Teaches

The essence of heaven and hell we carry within us.

Heaven and Hell

>Is heaven really up and hell down?
>Are heaven and hell really places?
>After death, does the body and/or soul
>truly travel to a place?
>Is that place a physical place that
>is up or down?

Heaven is certainly a positive image that we can conjure up in our minds. It is a place of peace and joy. It is a mystery that we will only understand when we have left this life…or is it?

Let's consider the possibility that the mystery of heaven includes everything from our conception to eternity. Heaven, or at least the creative force, is with us in our mother's womb. Heaven, or at least the powerful force of love, is with us as we choose a lifetime partner and have children. Heaven is with us in our caring and nurturing relationships every day.

But hell can also be with us in our everyday activities. The negative attitudes of anger, violence and hate are debilitating to our nature and can cause hell during our lifetime. This hell is part of our thinking because we have made the choice to live outside the bounds of unconditional love. Hell is in the distancing from God's love.

In the atmosphere of heaven, unconditional love will certainly prevail. Where love occurs in our daily life, we are already experiencing the nature of heaven. Heaven is in the presence of God.

Our thoughts and emotions are the keys to whether we experience heaven or hell from our conception to eternity. What a powerful responsibility that places on us when we are parents. As we raise our children, we have the opportunity to model for them unconditional love and all the essence of heaven. A positive role model does not guarantee that our children will experience heaven and unconditional love throughout their lives, but it increases the odds.

The Creator is certainly not restricted to a physical place. Therefore, it is hard to accept that heaven or hell are places. And, therefore, heaven and hell are not up and down.

Our essence, our soul, is our true being. Our present body is temporary. Therefore, our essence, our soul, can be eternal and not be restricted by the physical body.

When I experience my mother and father in my dreams, the fact that they died many years ago is of no importance. In my unconscious thought they are still in relationship with me and I with them. That will continue, I believe, even after my death. Our essence, our souls, can be together in a heavenly experience of love in our mortal life and after death.

Miracles and Mysteries

We don't understand many things that happen in our lives. The miracle of our lives is a mystery to us. Each of us has a unique fingerprint, a unique body and a unique soul. Like snowflakes, no two of us are alike. It is a miracle.

In our technology-oriented lives, we want to know why and how everything works. But can we explain why we are even on this earth? Why us? Why now? For what purpose?

The miracle of our life and the life of every newborn baby causes us to reflect on the miracle and the mystery of the Creator.

The more we wrestle with what we don't understand, the more we realize life has many mysteries that we were probably never made to understand—only experience.

Love is one of those incredible miracles and mysteries.

Love is a powerful experience. The more it is shared, the more everyone possesses.

Love is the true measure of effective human relations. We think of unconditional love and we are reminded of the guidance to "turn the other cheek" and "love your enemies."

The miracle of love is that self-centered human beings can find within their souls the teachings to love others.

The mystery of love is that its effects are very powerful to experience but are not quantitatively measurable.

God created us to love one another and gave us the divine messages of the soul within us to guide our decisions.

We live lives of miracles and mysteries, and that is our gift by the grace of God.

Where Love Resides

Love is an experience of great joy; when we love others we receive love ourselves.

The more love we give, the more love we get. Our mind is tuned to the positive power of love and is whole.

But where does love reside—in our heart, our mind or our soul?

The mystery of love is not for us to be anxious over, just to enjoy.

If love resides in our heart, our heart is full of joy as well as being the physical pump for our blood.

If love resides in our mind, our mind is enriched with positive experiences and memories.

If love resides in our soul, our soul becomes the true essence of our being and our positive power forever within us.

With love within our heart, our mind and our soul, we will experience love in the world.

The Simple Truth

To love and be loved; is it that simple?

We ponder the miracle of our life, from the power of the Universe to an egg, to a sperm, to our life.

Why are we here? What is our purpose in life?

What is our unique nature?

To love and be loved; is it that simple?

There is only one person who is on earth or ever was on earth or ever will be on earth who is me, and that is the me that I am.

Is my purpose in life to own a car, or a house, or land, or animals or forests?

Is my purpose to serve others or to manipulate situations to serve only my own desires?

To love and be loved; is it that simple?

When we come into this life as a baby and leave our bodily life in death, only our spirit is the constant.

Our form has changed over the years, our spirit has been nurtured and grown if we have loved and been loved.

It is important that we love ourselves as a unique child of God.

It is that simple. Our purpose in life is to love and be loved.

Everything else is secondary.

OUR DIALOG

Our inner observer is available to us for dialog and guidance. Our soul is our inner observer that we can call on at any time when we are seeking the teachings from our divine nature. Our soul includes our conscience.

Pause and Reflect

"I'm so busy, I can't think straight. Everything seems like a crisis. Days like this are no fun at all. So many people and so many events seem to require my time. There just aren't enough hours in the day."

It is extremely important to your Peace-of-Mind to periodically "Pause and Reflect." Consider this discussion with your inner observer:

Observer:
"It is good that you took a minute to pause and reflect about the situation. As you sense it, what's at the root of the situation?"

You:
"I just can't count on other people to do certain tasks, so I have to do them myself or they won't get done right."

Observer:
"You must have had some bad experiences with people in your life not following through on certain tasks."

You:
"Amen! And it's getting annoying doing so much work and not being recognized for it by management."

Observer:
"Have you considered various alternatives that could lead to your Peace-of-Mind?"

You:

"There are several alternatives, but they won't all lead to my Peace-of-Mind."

Observer:

"What are the alternatives, and which ones do you think are best for your Peace-of-Mind?"

You:

"I could just quit this job. But the anxiety of finding another one, which might not be any better, certainly wouldn't lead to my Peace-of-Mind."

Observer:

"Okay, that's one alternative that you have ruled out. How about the others?"

You:

"I could just emphasize the five most important projects on my desk and put off the other ten to later this week. That would give me some breathing room to not be quite so hassled."

Observer:

"Good, you have identified at least one alternative that can lead to more Peace-of-Mind. Are there others?"

You:

"Joe could help me on a few projects, but he has his job to do and I don't know how he'd respond if I asked him for help."

Observer:

"Would you be willing to help Joe on projects where you have the necessary skill?"

You:

"Sure, if I had the time. I guess the only way to find out if Joe has some time and is willing to help is to ask him."

Observer:

"That sounds reasonable; any other alternatives?"

You:

"I could take a little time out on Friday to better plan my work for the next week, so I don't get too many crisis projects on the same day."

Observer:

"That sounds reasonable."

You:

"I can't blame the clients; they deserve to have good service for the money they pay our company. I guess I feel better now that I've developed several alternatives that will lead to my Peace-of-Mind. Thanks for the help."

Observer:

"Contact me anytime. 'Pause and reflect' is a very useful tool."

Body and Soul

The bright white light is surrounding me; I've never experienced such a light of amazing intensity. I take my last earthly breath, and my soul separates from my body. My soul will live eternally, but my body is no longer a functioning temple for my soul.

Observer:
"Your essence, your soul, hasn't changed, but your body has died."
You:
"That is really strange; I pictured death as so much more final, but my soul continues to be joyous."

Observer:
"What is joyous for you now?"
You:
"There is no pain in my body. My spirit is free from the limits my body was imposing on me."

Observer:
"How are you feeling?"
You:
"Sad, yet free. Sad that the life I enjoyed in my body has come to an end, but free to experience the spiritual essence of my life."

Observer:
"What are your thoughts?"
You:
"For all my years, I thought my life was my body. Now, I realize that I am a spiritual being who spent part of my existence in that body of mine."

Observer:
"And what are your thoughts about your family?"
You:
"I am at peace now. I am together with the loved ones of my family who left the earthly life years ago. My friends and family who are still part of the earthly life understand that my soul is with them for eternity in their memories."

Observer:
"And, what of your tomorrows?"
You:
"Tomorrow is a new beginning. I have to learn again about my new life, just as I learned to crawl, walk and talk in my earthly life. It's a new and exhilarating experience."

Observer:
"Call me whenever you want to talk."
You:
"Thanks, it's good to have someone who can help me reflect on the important issues of my body and soul."

As the Soul Teaches

I prefer to be the more thoughtful, kind and understanding me — my true essence.

Observing Ourselves

Julia:

"The last two years in this job have made me into a different person. I've completely changed. My husband has noticed and I have noticed that I am just not at all like I was before."

Observer:

"That's fascinating. You feel you have become a truly different person in the last two years?"

Julia:

"Absolutely!"

Observer:

"May I ask, which person do you prefer to be—the old you or the current version of you?"

Julia:

"I prefer to be the old me, no question! I was much more thoughtful, kind and understanding. Now I'm angry and short-tempered a lot of the time."

Observer:

"If you prefer the old you—the thoughtful, kind and understanding you—what questions does that raise to you?"

Julia:

"Is this job driving me crazy the last few years? Or am I letting it affect me too much? Or what is really going on? Is it my boss?"

Observer:

"Do you have answers for those questions?"

Julia:

"Not this minute, but you have certainly jogged me to think out a very important subject. Thanks."

Observer:

"I'll be happy to chat with you anytime."

Tears of Sadness and Joy

Tears come to my eyes at weddings when I am so happy for the bride and groom.

The emotions of joy and happiness just naturally trigger the tear ducts to generate tears.

Tears—what a wonderful signal that our lives are rich with emotion.

A chorus can sing a beautiful song and my tears begin to flow.

A movie can have a touching scene of love or compassion and the tear ducts go to work.

What a wonder that our tears can originate with the emotions of joy, happiness, love or compassion.

But what of sadness and tears?

The same tear ducts generate tears from the stimulus of sadness.

At a funeral, we cry when our brain is wrestling with the relationship that was and the new reality of death.

Years after a time of sadness, if we focus our thoughts on the sad incident, our emotions go to work and the tears flow.

A broken relationship is a sad happening, and tears remind us of what might have been.

Those who have cried often have lived richly.

To not have cried is to have controlled the emotions so much as to deny their reality.

As the Soul Teaches

Tears are a great cleanser. They cleanse the eyes and the soul.

Tears are a wonderful gift from God—tears of sadness and joy; tears of a full rich life.

As the Soul Teaches

Peace-of-Mind is ours as we ponder difficult moral issues.

Legal, Amoral and Moral Behavior

Slavery was once legal in the United States, but in the broad view that all human beings are equal in the eyes of their Creator, slavery was immoral. It was immoral to treat human beings as objects to be bought and sold by other human beings.

It was legal once that women did not have the right to vote in the United States, but in the broad view that all human beings are equal in the eyes of their Creator, prohibiting women from voting was immoral.

- Morality is defined in the dictionary as upright conduct.
- Moral is defined as relating to principles of right and wrong; being virtuous.
- Amoral is defined as behavior that is indifferent to morality.
- Immoral is defined as violating accepted standards of moral behavior.

Therefore, certain behavior may be viewed as legal in the context of society at the time, but such behavior need not be considered moral.

In Germany and throughout Europe, Hitler promoted the immoral killing of Jews and others under the cover of legal authority from the German government. It was far too serious to consider those decisions as amoral; they clearly were immoral.

But lest we make every decision a moral decision, there are some amoral decisions:

1. Shall I purchase vanilla or chocolate ice cream?
2. Shall I purchase a large or small car?
3. Shall I live in the city or the country?
4. Shall I marry or remain single?

Let's consider some difficult areas of moral judgment:

Euthanasia

Euthanasia is the deliberate killing of persons who suffer from a painful and incurable disease or condition (sometimes called mercy killing).

Murder is considered immoral. Euthanasia involves killing someone who chooses to die. Is God the only power to decide when a person is to die, or do people have the moral right to kill themselves or have someone kill them to end their suffering?

It is my belief that suicide, murder and euthanasia are not God's will for us. We are on this earth because the Creator put us here. We should die in God's good time, not our own. Perhaps we have more to contribute as a live person.

Withholding Medical Care

Some people have decided not to provide their child with medical care on the basis that their religion prohibits such care and requires that the only acceptable route for healing the child is divine intervention. Is God the only power to decide when a person is to die? Does the person or parents have the moral right to withhold medical care? In my view, withholding medical care is not God's will for us.

Societies have their different cultural ways of resolving such moral puzzles. Some bring the decision through the legal process to decide what is right or wrong. Some defer to the person of ultimate authority in the society (the Chief, the King, and so on who, presumably, they feel is most in tune with the will of God or the force they consider most powerful).

But how is an individual to make these types of difficult moral decisions? I submit that Peace-of-Mind will come to those who honestly ponder on the difficult moral issues of their life by seeking the counsel of their inner observer, which is a part of their essence provided to them by their Creator. Some call this prayer or meditation.

Fred:
"My pain is horrible. I have lived long enough. I wish I would just not wake up tomorrow."

Observer:
"I understand your pain. Are there any good parts of your life that make life worth living?"

Fred:
"The pain makes everything in life miserable."

Observer:
"Are there any people you love and who love you whom

you should consider?"

Fred:
"Well, there is my son, my niece and an old golfing buddy who at least come to visit me once in a while."

Observer:
"Maybe it would be good if you gave those three people a call and told them you'd love to see them soon because you are feeling rather depressed."

Fred:
"Good idea. I'll give them each a call."

Observer:
"Contact me anytime when you have serious topics that you need to discuss. That's why I am here for you."

Moral decisions involve our conscience, our soul, our very essence. We need to reach to our inner observer and to our loved ones for help when we are facing moral questions.

War and Peace

Mother Theresa guided many people toward loving and peaceful goals. Her advice often was "Begin by loving your family and caring for them." Albert Einstein said, "It is impossible to simultaneously prepare for peace and for war."

Each of us has to decide where peace and war begins and ends for us as individuals. Jesus said, "Blessed are the peacemakers for they shall be called sons of God."

Yet wars occur time and time again—little wars (like one person knifing or shooting another) and big wars (organized hate by one large group for another with possession of the other's land and riches often the goal).

The sources of war are the baser natures of humanity—hate, greed, violence and selfishness. Peace requires unconditional love.

Peace-of-Mind and peace on earth both stem from the same attitude of unconditional love. Turning the other cheek is very difficult for humans to do; it is our best guidance from our soul that encourages unconditional love.

We live in an unusual time in the world where the United States is the acknowledged major world military power. Fortunately, the United States has generally used its power for moral purposes. Terrorists and local wars will occur. Beatings and shootings will occur on the local scene. Punishment for crimes is absolutely necessary to deter crime. Yet unconditional love must always be analyzed as the guideline from our soul.

As the Soul Teaches

Tapping the Unconscious

Our dreams and imagination are as real a part of our being as our conscious thoughts. Our soul is involved in all our levels of consciousness.

Dreaming

Which thought is more real—one that occurs in our conscious mind, our subconscious mind or in our unconscious mind? Scientists have concluded that only about 15% of our thoughts occur in our conscious mind. Are the other 85% of our thoughts not important? Should we ignore those 85% of our thoughts?

Meditation, reverie, daydreaming, night dreaming—where do these thoughts come from? Of course, when we just analyze a bit, we conclude that we are the author, scriptwriter, producer, and director of all our thoughts and dreams. No matter how amazing our thoughts and dreams are to our conscious mind, we created all of those thoughts and dreams.

Our soul is involved in every single one of our thoughts, conscious and unconscious. The Creator has given us a free will to decide to listen to the messages of our soul or only the messages of the world. Peace-of-Mind is ours when we follow the guidance of our soul. But it is so hard. First, we must listen to all our thoughts from conscious to unconscious, and then we must sort out the messages that we want to follow.

We are called to love, but our thoughts often lead us to hate and anger until we listen more carefully to our soul and tune ourselves to the best that is within us.

Our dreams and imagination are as real a part of our being as our conscious thought. We can unleash the power of our creativity, dreams and imagination to influence our conscious thought and behavior.

As the Soul Teaches

Our soul sings and we need to play the tune to accompany the soaring of our soul. We are the vehicle for our soul to become a major influence for good, love and peace in our world. Only through our cooperation and free will can our soul have the maximum impact that the Creator gives us as unique individuals.

We wake from a dream which seemed, and was, so real.

The Dreams of Your Life

Let's analyze where dreams come from—both daydreams and night dreams—and what they can mean to us.

First, I believe we have four techniques that are available to us to find God's will for our lives—prayer, meditation, life's experiences, and dreams. God guides our lives and we have the free will to listen and follow or to not tune in at all.

About 15% of our thought is conscious thought, so 85% is subconscious or unconscious. That is such a huge part of our being that it is worth studying. I studied at Brooklyn Technical High School, in Brooklyn, New York, and the Massachusetts Institute of Technology, in Cambridge, Massachusetts. I was trained to think analytically and logically using the left side of my brain. For the past forty years, I have been learning about and experiencing the wonders of the right side of the brain—intuition, fantasy, imagination and the wonders of the subconscious and unconscious thinking processes. Everything is important because we are one being, one essence.

Science has found that our bodies' cells are completely replaced by new cells every few years. As the cells change, the infant grows to a child, the child grows to an adult and the adult ages. We are blessed with a fabulous body, but our essence is more than the body—it is our spirit.

We wake from a dream and the dream seemed so real. People were in our dream who have been dead for dozens of years. Where did that very real dream come from? It came from our subconscious mind, which has many stored memories and fantasies. We heard and saw the story of the dream, but we were also the scriptwriter and director of the dream. It was a happy or sad dream because we produced it to be that way in our brain.

Dreams are so fascinating to me that I have studied them for many years via workshops, books, and my own experiences. Some dreams are fairly straightforward—getting lost, frustrated, unable to get to a place you want to get to (not able to find a classroom or your books or a locker), being able to fly, or fulfilling a fantasy.

The mechanism of remembering my dreams has been amazing to me. When I wake at night with a dream, I write it down on a pad by my bed. It's amazing how more of the dream comes to my mind as I write—people, things, colors, actions. I say to myself, "Then this happened, and then…oh yes, and then this, then this." It seems that the unconscious thoughts of the dream are moving to my conscious mind, and from there they direct my hand to do the writing. Then the unconscious sends some more messages to the subconscious and to my conscious mind with the next section of the dream. It is very common that I'll then recall another dream and another dream. Six to eight completely different dreams surface in the fifteen minutes I am taking to write them down as fast as I can write. It is a very exciting and rewarding experience.

Then in the morning, I get the treat of recording the latest group of dreams and reading the others from the night. There is no way that I would have remembered the dreams if

I hadn't recorded them immediately upon awaking. If I use a radio alarm to wake, the radio's music or words bring me into the regular world so quickly that the dream world fades away. So 99% of the time, I choose to wake without an alarm so I can recall my dreams.

For a month or two I'll record all my dreams. Then I'll take a vacation from dream journaling and return later. It is fun to utilize the feedback from the brain's activity.

Analyzing dreams is a personal activity. My dreams are very rich and very fascinating to analyze. Yours are too, if you choose to study them.

Amazingly, it is possible to influence your dreams and change the story, the direction and the conclusions while the dream is going on. That shouldn't be too surprising, because after all, you are the scriptwriter (perhaps with God's help from the divine spirit within you).

Life is so rich, all 24 hours of every day, that we should enjoy all of it.

But sometimes dreams are scary or sad or disturbing. There is a dark side to our dreams sometimes because we are human. With joy in our life, there is also some sadness. Facing the dark side and analyzing it for your growth can be as rewarding as enjoying the fun fantasies of your dreams.

All our experiences are part of our life's conscious, subconscious, and unconscious thinking. We should consider enjoying the joy, analyzing and learning from the sadness and following the lessons we learn from our mind, our heart and our essence.

Every Dream Has a Meaning

One morning I woke up at 3:00 a.m. and recalled that I had been dreaming a number of different dreams. I decided to record my memories of them in some detail.

In one dream I recalled having a yellow-lined pad and writing three sentences on it—one at the top of the page, one in the center and one at the bottom. What were these words? I challenged myself, and the following three statements were the result of my journaling:

- Love and caring in a relationship comes from being non-judgmental, not criticizing others and always being supportive of others.
- Love and caring in an organization or society comes from treating people with kindness, dignity and respect.
- Love and caring for yourself is the cornerstone of your relationship with others.

I've treasured these words ever since as guidance from my soul.

In another dream, my mother and sister, both of whom have been in heaven for years, were sitting on the living room sofa of the home I lived in for my first sixteen years. But the peculiar part of the dream was that they were both completely nude. My mother was about thirty-five in the dream and my sister about five, which was reasonable since my sister was born on my mother's thirtieth birthday. I had never seen my mother or sister nude, but that was the dream.

Every dream has a meaning. I have attended workshops and read extensively about dreams so that I can attempt to analyze my dreams. I don't try to analyze anyone else's dreams. My analysis of this dream was quite comforting. My mother and sister had very pink skin and cherubic round faces in the dream. My conclusion was that they were together in heaven now where clothes were not needed because there is no sense of shame and there is no need for warmth from clothing. What started out as a strange dream, once I thought it through, was a comforting message from my soul. I was content that my mind had concluded that they were at peace in heaven with God and each other. And I concluded that in God's time, I would be able to join them in eternal peace.

Musings of a Runner

Left, right, left, right, left, right, left, right.

"It sure is cold this morning. I'm glad I put on plenty of layers of clothes. This ski cap and these mittens are perfect for today. Looks like there are some ice patches under the blown snow—take it a little easy."

Left, right, left, right, left, right, left, right.

"That dream I had last night was really special. It started in a rehabilitation hospital or a nursing home with dozens of people of all ages on crutches or in wheelchairs. It was a sad scene until the music started and got real peppy. One by one, the crutches were being raised until everyone on crutches was putting them forward and then up above their heads. They were all dancing without the use of their crutches. In fact, they were swirling their crutches up and down and around to the beat of the music. The sadness was gone and all the men and women were smiling. I didn't see any children. And then the people in wheelchairs started zooming around the room and bumping each other like children in bumper cars at a carnival."

Left, right, left, right, left, right, left, right.

"My goodness, the geese are still around and it's January. Usually they have gone south by Thanksgiving. The creek is almost frozen solid so it won't be long before they leave for warmer weather. But they'll be back. By May we'll have hundreds of yellow puffs of fur with the next generation of goslings. Here it is January and the goslings have all grown to be as large as their parents. I can't tell which ones are the parents out of the roughly thirty total. How do they know when it's time to fly south? Instinct?"

Left, right, left, right, left, right, left, right.

"Decision time. I guess I'll take the long route through the park today. I'm feeling good and I've warmed up even though the air temperature is below zero."

Left, right, left, right, left, right, left, right.

"What should I get my wife for her birthday? It's only a week before Valentine's Day. I can't decide. Guess I'll just give that job to my unconscious mind. Unconscious, go to work on that while I think about something else."

Left, right, left, right, left, right, left, right.

"Look at those children playing hockey on the ice rink. Wow, is that ice smooth. They hit the puck and it goes so far on the smooth ice. I bet our grandchildren would love to play on that ice. They don't have skates yet, but we could pull them on a sled or have them push a chair along on the ice to keep their balance as they pretend to skate. Unconscious, remember that idea for me until later."

Left, right, left, right, left, right, left, right.

"People dancing in a rehabilitation center, isn't that great? Perhaps they are dancing to the music in their souls, even though their bodies aren't cooperating. Our spirit is so much stronger than our body. I guess that's why our spirit is our true essence and our eternal part."

Left, right, left, right, left, right, left, right.

"I forgot to call my son last night. Subconscious, remind me to do that tonight."

Left, right, left, right, left, right, left, right.

"I wonder how long geese live. They all look alike to me. I wonder if there are any grandparents in that flock or if the grandparents stay in the south. Generations of geese, like generations of humans. Complete with instincts built in by their Creator and open to training by their parents. Parenting really is a big responsibility for all of God's creatures. I'll have to strive to do a better job of parenting. At least I should call my son tonight."

Left, right, left, right, left, right, left, right.

And Then, I Prayed

"Dear God, help me handle this stressful situation. Give me patience, strength, and courage. Amen."

When you pray, are you talking to a God who is in heaven or the God who is within you every day in your soul? Is it a close personal conversation or a distant one?

If you believe that people were created in the image of God, then there is a divine element in your being. Whether your divine essence is a part of your brain, your heart, your soul or whatever, that is your spiritual perception and reality.

We live as conscious beings, but we also have subconscious and unconscious reality, which is part of our life. The messages we receive in our dreams come from within us. We are the authors and directors of our dreams. Perhaps this is one way the divine essence, which is within us, communicates to us. Do we follow the divine messages?

Are prayers answered? If we pray for strength and courage, our prayers have a good chance of being answered. We can help influence our own future by what we think. How we pray and how we listen to the voice guiding us from within is critical to our attitude toward prayer and answered prayers.

Prayer and meditation are important techniques for seeking to attain Peace-of-Mind. It is worth reflecting on how we think about prayer and its power in our lives.

Some say, "Let go, let God" as a technique for sharing burdens with a spiritual power within each of us that is often much more capable of Peace-of-Mind than our conscious selves.

As the Soul Teaches

Re-parenting; tapping into our true inner being, the self we choose to be.

Re-Parenting Ourselves

We don't get to choose our parents. However, we do have a free will and can elect to re-parent ourselves if we are unhappy with the parenting we received from our parents.

Some people would find this statement shocking—they'd say, "Certainly we are stuck with what we received as children from our parents." That is a victim mentality.

One of the powerful workshops that I participated in on re-parenting ourselves has had a lasting impact on my life. I'd like to share the main concepts of the workshop with you.

- All around the room were dozens of charts with many hundreds of comments a child could hear from his or her parents while growing up (positive and negative). "You're great. I wish you were dead. I love you. You drive me crazy. I never want to see you again. You are a wonderful dancer. Get out of this house. You deserve better than I have given you. Thank you. Go straight to hell. You're just like your father—no good."

- Each workshop participant was then asked to take ten small pieces of paper and record the ten comments they most remembered from their youth (whether positive or negative). The many statements on the wall charts were useful to give the workshop participants some specific examples to stimulate their memories about their own youth and to help them write down the ten most remembered messages.

- After everyone had written down ten comments, the facilitator explained how some people may have two positive messages and eight negatives while others may have seven positives and three negatives, but each person is expected only to reflect on his or her own ten.

- After the facilitator's comments, the workshop participants were told that they could select the comments from their parents that they wanted to change. The change could be written in their own words. To close the loop, the facilitator gave us the power to crush the parenting message we didn't want and toss it aggressively onto the floor as we replaced it with words we'd prefer.

- After the purge of the unwanted comments and rewriting them to what we'd prefer, each workshop participant now had the opportunity to review the ten messages and accept them as his or her new parenting messages.

Reflecting anew on this workshop, I believe the power in it is the power we find within ourselves...from our soul. The workshop gave us permission to address subjects that we had accepted as the "givens" in our lives. Now, with the simple authority of the workshop facilitator, we can feel empowered by writing new parenting messages for ourselves.

Also, we get to confirm those messages we appreciated from our parents and allow our soul to appreciate and accept them.

No longer can we say, "My mother always said…" or "My father treated me like…" without recognizing that we have the free will given to us by our Creator to accept or reject our parent's messages to us. Re-parenting ourselves is hard work, but it is well worth the effort for our Peace-of-Mind.

Re-parenting ourselves is a useful approach for tapping into our true inner being, the self we choose to be. We can do it by listening to our soul's messages without the necessity of a workshop experience.

Our Emotions

Our emotions are ours; they come from within us. No one can directly make us happy, sad, angry, furious or crazy.

Others may have certain behavior patterns and use certain words.

But only we can control our own emotions.

Peace-of-Mind and good mental health require that we have a filter, which we apply to what we experience, and only after applying the filter do we decide what our emotions will be to each outside stimulus.

My emotions are mine and are valid.

I am responsible for all of my own emotions.

We have choices to make in life, and one very critical choice is to accept full responsibility for our own emotions.

It is a choice of self-empowerment and a choice for Peace-of-Mind.

AS THE SOUL TEACHES

LIFE'S GUIDEPOSTS

Our soul helps us each create an exciting and rewarding path for our life.

The Flow of Life

> Our first home is our mother's womb—
> safe, comfortable and nurturing.
> Our final home is heaven for eternity-
> safe, comfortable and nurturing.
> We live life between womb and eternity
> in a series of environments that we call home.

Our physical needs are all provided for us in the womb and in eternity. In the womb and in eternity we have the ultimate Peace-of-Mind. Clothing, transportation, and money have no meaning in the womb or in eternity.

What is constant for all of our earthly and heavenly existence is the uniqueness of our soul. In the eyes of God, we began unique and always will be unique as individuals.

We begin life as part of a family, and by the time our soul abides in heaven, we have experienced many positive and negative relationships—times of love, times of hate, times of nurturing, times of anger, times of togetherness, times of separation. If we have learned well as our soul has taught us over the years, we have experienced Peace-of-Mind through all of life. We can then share the peace of heaven with all our friends and relatives who are already in eternity.

Our possessions (our car, our house, our furniture, our stocks, our bonds, and on and on) have importance to the physical comfort of our lives but have no relevance in the womb or in eternity. Yet so much of our life is spent with concerns about possessions. Peace-of-Mind is ours when we listen to the teachings of our soul that tell us possessions are ours to enjoy and to share with others. Too much focus on possessions can emphasize the physical nature of our being over the spiritual and emotional nature of our being and make us unbalanced.

To love and to be loved, those are the critical parts of the Peace-of-Mind we can enjoy. Our mission in life, guided by the teachings of our soul, is to love and be loved.

And God spoke to Roberta, "Welcome to the eternal peace which I promised you. Welcome my good and faithful servant." And Roberta was amazed. "I can't imagine a life in heaven; I'm just not prepared for it," she said. "And what would your wish be?" said God. "I wish," said Roberta, "that I could live my earthly life over again, but with the perspective of the eternal peace that I now know is ahead." "Your wish is granted, but with one important twist," said God. "You will begin your new life on earth as an eighty-nine-year-old woman on her death bed and end it as an embryo in your mother's womb, and then you will return to join me again in eternal peace."

St. Mary's hospital was at the center of town, across the street from a large hotel and a shopping center. On the fourth floor of the intensive care unit, Roberta was opening her eyes to see her family members around her. "You know, I'm feeling a little better," she said. "It's amazing," said her son, "I thought you had gone to sleep a few minutes ago."

And, with her new perspective, Roberta became a miracle to her community, friends and family. Her body strengthened and she was able to return to the nursing home where she had lived before her final visit to the hospital.

The doctors and her family were amazed at her renewed vigor—she was a regular hotrod in her wheelchair until they returned her to her old home. Each day and each year she got younger and more vigorous. She was back to walking and even jogging, and her body was now the body of a sixty-year-old woman. But what of her soul?

"My soul soars to the mountaintops when I realize that it was trapped in a physical body that wasn't functioning too well. My soul always has been teaching me to love unconditionally, but now I fully understand that loving and being loved was and is my primary purpose on earth. Praise be to God."

And the years progressed as Roberta got younger. She enjoyed her children as they progressed from adulthood to childhood to their spectacular births. And Roberta proclaimed, "Getting younger is a fabulous experience and looking at the world through younger eyes each day, my friends and family, is a rich gift."

And Roberta progressed to the teenage years where she had a new perspective of her parents. Roberta, after all, had reached her teenage years after being a mother herself, an adult, a grandmother and an eighty-nine-year-old woman. Now, as a teenager, she could bring a perspective to everyday life that her friends could only imagine.

And Roberta was soon a toddler, playing with toys with her brother and her father. "What a rich experience it is to grow young," she thought.

And then to return to the womb of her mother where life was safe, comfortable and nurturing. What a full rich life she had lived from conception to eighty-nine years old and back to conception again.

And Roberta returned to be with God. She said, "Life and afterlife have a whole new perspective for me. No matter what stage my physical body was in, my soul was with me always, teaching me all the way. Praise be to you, my Creator."

The Real Facts of Life

We are on this earth to be in relationship with each other and with our Creator.

Relationships can range from love to hate and every possibility between.

It is intellectually and emotionally hard to accept that our Creator intends us to live in relationships of hate, anger, fear, or violence.

Rather, we expect that our Creator intends us to live in relationships of love, harmony, mutual support and peace.

Then how do we explain a world of so many relationships between people that are of hate, anger, fear or violence?

It must be that we have been given a free will by our Creator to choose between good and evil, love and hate, harmony and anger, mutual support and fear, peace and violence.

As parents, our greatest gifts to our family are the real facts of life; our total purpose is to love and be loved, to live in positive relationships and to resist all negative forces.

Our Creator has given us a soul and a divine spirit within us to guide us to wise choices in life.

The real facts of life are within us to tune into and develop into the best person we can be.

As the Soul Teaches

We are all family; no human is a foreigner.

"Family" Rather Than "Foreigner"

All humans on earth are related and have common ancestors.

Whether the ancestors were Adam and Eve or whoever, history is clear that the species we call human beings have a common heritage.

We live in different parts of the planet, have different skin pigmentation, speak different languages and have different social customs.

Yet, as we trace back our family tree, we find that we are related to people from all parts of our country and other countries.

So who is a foreigner? Is a foreigner a person who was born in some country other than the one where we were born?

Perhaps the country of our birth should not be considered as important as the fact that all human beings have many similar characteristics and even similar DNA.

We all were created by the same Creator.

We are all family in the true sense of the word.

Therefore, a better word than foreigner might be family.

We love our family members. We consider them special and they love us in return.

We are part of God's family of human beings on earth. What a positive perspective: "family" rather than "foreigner."

Leadership

Followers define who will be their leaders.

If we choose to accept the leadership of an individual, we have accepted the principles and vision of that individual.

If we disagree with the principles and vision of a leader, we are meeting our needs and the needs of society by picking a new leader.

Hitler was a leader, for evil, and many followed.

Ghandi was a leader, for good, and many followed.

Gang members have followers who steal and kill to be accepted as members of the gang and as loyal supporters of the leader.

Military leaders can use their power for good or for evil.

Loyalty to a leader of character, honesty and moral principle is wise and noble.

Loyalty to a leader who is evil decreases the moral fiber of the followers.

Leadership must be earned by the steady support of the followers.

Therefore, we get the quality of leadership we deserve in business, government…in all society.

If we want better leaders, we need to be guided as followers to align ourselves only with leaders of character, honesty and moral principle.

As the Soul Teaches

When no one is looking, except our soul.

Integrity

To tell the truth or to lie, that is the question.

A person of integrity is a person who you can trust to be honest, to tell the truth.

People without integrity are people whom you can't trust because you are not sure when they will be honest and when they will be dishonest.

Integrity is the core of a successful marriage.
Only if you can trust your partner do you feel comfortable in sharing your most private thoughts.

Integrity is the core of a successful business.
When a company makes promises to provide certain products or services with certain assurances, they must deliver on those promises or lose clients.

Integrity is the core of a lasting friendship.
We trust a friend who has demonstrated time and again that he or she is trustworthy.

When we accept lack of honesty or clear dishonesty, we are accepting a lack of integrity without questioning.

The person who has exhibited a lack of integrity can feel somewhat justified because his or her dishonesty was not challenged.

Consider a child who is dishonest many times with his parents and is allowed to not pay any consequences.

The child begins to conclude that the world is that way; he or she can be dishonest and it is accepted.

This is not the message we want to convey to our children as we help them to mature in body and spirit.

Love is embedded in expecting integrity.

To accept dishonesty, lying or lack of integrity is to miss the lessons of love.

Love and truth must be connected.

That's how marriages and relationships survive and grow. Integrity is critical to every relationship of respect and love.

The Truth, the Whole Truth, and Nothing but the Truth

The justice system asks people to pledge to give "the truth, the whole truth and nothing but the truth."

And yet, we know that lawyers have rehearsed the people testifying, to have the right words said. Why?

If what is wanted is the whole truth and nothing but the truth, a person need only be honest to their soul and everyone else. Right?

Truth should be our friend. In our justice system, we have an adversarial approach (one side prosecuting, the other side defending).

Truth is not the goal in our justice system, but rather winning, convincing the judge, or convincing the jury.

If a person is found not guilty of a situation when, in truth, he was guilty, he can conclude that he defeated the justice system and is personally above the law.

But, every minute of every day such a person must live with his conscience and his soul, knowing that he lied and violated his oath. God knows the truth, and so does the guilty person.

And what of the person who is found guilty, when, in truth, he was innocent? Then the administrators of the justice system, the lawyers, the judges and the jury, have been faulty in the pursuit of justice.

Is truth really so relative that the people who have the highest paid lawyers generally prevail? What a cynical thought.

Our best ally is the teachings of our soul. We must live with our soul for eternity. Yes, for eternity.

We know the truth and our soul teaches us to be truthful. God knows the truth, and so do we.

Peace-of-Mind comes from telling the truth. Peace-of-Mind is a wonderful treasure from our soul when we are truthful at all times.

The Moral Compass

How is a person to know what is evil and what is good?

A newborn child does not know the difference between good and evil, so it is something we must learn in life.

Who will our teachers be? Our parents, certainly. Probably our friends and neighbors. Our teachers in school, likely. And hopefully our religious leaders.

Can we also learn ourselves? By experiencing life and analyzing situations compared to what we have learned to be good and evil, moral and immoral?

Our religious training is often a very helpful partner for our parents as they gradually educate us on right and wrong, good and evil.

In some faiths there are commandments to define good and evil. Thou shalt and thou shalt not.

Our soul is the moral compass for our conscience.

As we enrich the soul with what is good, and educate our soul to abhor evil, our conscience is perfected.

We are made in the image of God and, therefore, there is a divinity within us.

That divine spirit within us is a moral compass that guides our soul in all decisions of good and evil.

Praise be to God.

As the Soul Teaches

Play to live, live to play.

Let's Play

Imagine yourself as a five-year-old child, or one of your children at age five, or one of your grandchildren at age five.

Play is a wonderful experience for all humans at every age. If only we could play all our life with the zest for life of a five-year-old child.

Play is a spontaneous pleasure that God has given us to enjoy alone and with others.

When we play alone, with the creativity and imagination of a five-year-old child, we can talk to our stuffed dog and have a great two-way conversation.

We can build a castle with our blocks, knock it down and giggle, build it up again a different way and cheer.

We can build a fort between the chair and the sofa, with a blanket for a roof, and we can bring our truck and favorite seashells into the secret corner of our fort.

When we play with others, sometimes we play school. Isn't it fascinating that the oldest child always chooses to be the teacher?

And we play a card game with our mommy and daddy; it's fun to win but a little sad to lose. When we lose, we want to play a different game.

Playing in the bathtub is always fun with the plastic fish, the yellow rubber ducky and the little boat. We can pretend we are in the ocean swimming with the big fish and the big boats.

We build a snowman in the winter, watch the baby robins in their nest in the spring, roll on the grass in the summer and jump in the piles of leaves in the fall.

And our soul soars with glee as we play at all ages. What a wonderful gift from God, our ability to play, laugh and imagine.

As humans, play is part of our wonderful gift from our Creator. Let's play from now to eternity.

Creative Living

Youth is not a time of life but a state of mind. It is a temper of the will—a quality of the imagination—a vigor of the emotions.

Nobody grows old by merely living a number of years.

People grow old only by deserting their ideals.

Years wrinkle the skin, but to give up enthusiam wrinkles the soul.

Worry, doubt, self-distrust, fear and despair—these are the long, long years that bow the heart and turn the greening spirit back to dust.

Whether eight or eighty, there is in very human being's heart the lure of wonder, the undaunted challenge of events, the unfailing child-like appetite for what next, and the joy of the game of living.

We are as young as our self-confidence, as old as our fear, as young as our desire, as old as our despair.

OUR BEHAVIOR

Our spirituality influences our daily decisions and behavior in society. This section of the book on our behavior is a change of perspective from all other sections. Everyday decisions in our personal life and in the business world are addressed. This section is about the practical applications that result in our lives from the impact of our spiritual foundation and the teachings of the soul.

Finding Your Calling

At age fifteen and sixteen, I was very active in the youth group of Good Shepherd Lutheran Church in Brooklyn, New York. I recall giving sermons on Youth Sunday and receiving very positive feedback from the adults. A group of the youth choir members and I occasionally conducted the service for old congregations in New York that had dwindled in numbers and could no longer afford a full-time minister. The choir and I would conduct the full service and I would present the sermon.

At age eighteen, after a year of studying chemical engineering at Massachusetts Institute of Technology, in Cambridge, Massachusetts, I conducted the service again at Good Shepherd as a college student home for the summer. I can recall the sermon that I gave clearly. It was about a plus sign with the discussion of the vertical line as ones relationship to God and the horizontal line as ones relationship to all human beings. My sister, who was six years older than me and married with a child, came up to me after the service and said, "Bill, are you sure you want to be an engineer? Maybe you should consider being a minister." My sister and I had an interesting relationship—she was more like a junior mother than a playmate. She died, as it turned out, when she was forty-three. I've communed with her since in my dreams.

With my sister's comments about my possibly going into the ministry as a profession on my mind, I did some serious soul searching that summer. I decided to return to M.I.T. in the fall and continue to study chemical engineering but always to seek opportunities in my life to serve and to minister in my work and all my relationships. I had the opportunity to become an ordained elder of the Presbyterian Church in Virginia and have served on the layperson's board of four churches over the years while teaching adult Sunday school for many years.

Career selection is a challenging task for a young person.

Who calls? Does the Creator call us?

Who responds? Do we do so reluctantly or willingly?

How do we find our purpose in life, our calling?

"Finding your calling" is another way of saying "finding God's will for your life." That's not something that happens easily for most people. Most people, I submit, move from job to job, lifestyle to lifestyle, relationship to relationship without ever consciously asking the question of themselves, "What is God's will for me?"

Many practical people feel that we make decisions on a pleasure-pain scale. Most decisions are based, this concept suggests, on maximizing pleasure and minimizing pain.

If some people don't swim well, they perceive that being a swimming coach or a competitive swimmer is very painful. They elect to teach if they perceive that will give them pleasure in educating young people.

Therefore, people will tend to work at the type of work they do fairly well and play the types of sports they play fairly well rather than living through long periods of pain pursuing something they don't enjoy.

But even pursuing a field of endeavor a person enjoys can require many years of persistence and dedication before the person begins to be quite successful. If the end goal is attractive, people will bear some pain to attain the goal that brings them pleasure in the long run.

To search one's soul is critical to guide the decisions of selecting your life's work, your lifelong partner, your ultimate goals in life, and so on. Peace-of-Mind is available after a careful, analytical analysis is made (left brain) and a thorough exploration of imagination, fantasy and intuition (right brain) is completed.

Ultimately, life is a trial-and-error process. We decide, we change our plan, we decide differently, the situations in our life alter, we decide again and again. It is much like a sailboat moving across a body of water by sometimes having the wind helping dramatically and sometimes having to tack back and forth into the wind to reach the direction from which the wind is blowing.

We should not expect smooth sailing all the time. No wind and it seems as though we can't progress in any direction. Storms approach and we are afraid for our lives, for even trying to move to the other side of the body of water.

But perhaps the creative solution is to have a spiritual motor on board to help when the wind seems to be thwarting us.

Through self-analysis, meditation and seeking the messages from our soul, we can obtain guidance on finding our calling. It doesn't just happen. Conscious attention to carefully seeking many options is essential to our decision making, especially in those times when critical decisions are necessary.

As the Soul Teaches

The best that is within us and Peace-of-Mind will emerge if we listen to the teaching of our soul.

A Person's Mindset

If you are a person who sees a glass of water as half-full, it is said that you are an optimist. It is said that the pessimist considers the glass half-empty.

A person's mindset is strongly influenced by his or her experiences in life from childhood to the present. The mindset is established over a long period of time and, therefore, is not easily changed. A mindset can be changed, but only with a concerted effort by a person to reprogram his or her mind. Reprogramming takes dedication and time.

In my experience over the years, people who are not trustworthy are generally the ones who don't trust others. They believe others are out to take advantage of them because that is their mindset. (Do unto others before they do unto you.)

A wise realtor once summarized this concept for me as "people who question others as having hidden agendas often have hidden agendas of their own."

TRUST

To trust is to bond with another person
with great confidence and pleasure.

A person you can trust knows that they can trust you
and your word to be honest and fair.

Trust is a mutual respect and allegiance
based on sincere good will.

We are cautious about whom we trust, and it is healthy
to test boundaries to avoid being hurt.

When we have found someone not to have been trustworthy,
we may take quite a while to trust them again.
Trust must be earned through
consistency and predictability.

A bond of friendship is to be treasured
when it includes a bond of unconditional trust.

Those we can trust are those with whom we want to spend
time and who make us feel good about ourselves.

As the Soul Teaches

We are all related as members of God's family.

A Potential Giant Step Toward Tolerance

All human beings on earth are related with common ancestors. Therefore, we are all family in the true sense of the word.

Suppose in the next census a person with a mother of Chinese heritage and a father of Irish heritage is asked to categorize himself for the census taker. Does he check the Caucasian box, the Asian box or what? There are no places for percentages. I submit that this is reality and it is wrong to even ask the question that requires that a person label himself or herself for the record.

Tiger Woods was praised as the first African-American to win the Masters golf tournament. Over time, he politely pointed out that his heritage was Caucasian, Black, Asian and Indian, which might make him a Caublasian. Do we need rules on what percentage of each race or ethnic background a person is? Of course not, just eliminate the offensive labeling question from the 2000 census and all census taking in the future.

I was born in Brooklyn, New York, and Jackie Robinson was one of my heroes when he joined the Brooklyn Dodgers to play major league baseball in 1947. As a twelve-year-old child, baseball was an important part of my life. I learned to copy Jackie's technique of standing at bat and tapping his right thigh with his right hand several times before each pitch. I was told by the radio announcers that Jackie was so good at stealing bases because he ran pigeon-toed, which made him run faster. (He had also been a track star at college.) So, as a youngster following his role model, I tried to run faster by running pigeon-toed. I loved how enthusiastic Jackie Robinson was about baseball, and when my dad brought me to Ebbetts Field to see the Dodgers play, Jackie was the one I cheered for the most. Why? Because he was a great ballplayer! It was not a plus or a minus to me that his skin was black and mine was white.

General Colin Powell tells the story of being complimented by a superior officer that he was "the best black Lieutenant in the Army." General Powell preferred to have been praised for being the best Lieutenant, independent of his skin color.

Oddly, we don't say Sammy Sosa hit the most home runs in 1998 of all the dark-skinned players and Mark McGuire hit the most home runs in 1998 of all the light-skinned players. We need to honor the best home run hitter. Their skin color has absolutely nothing to do with their accomplishment.

No one says Michael Jordan is the best black basketball player of all time; we just say he's the best. His skin color has nothing to do with his skills and accomplishments.

It is time to draw the line and declare that we are taking a census of all Americans. We are not going to keep track of what percent of what ethnic or racial group we have in 1990 vs. 2000 vs. 2010. Why should we? The labels are incorrect anyhow because we all have a common heritage. Our skin color, culture and language when our ancestors arrived in the United States has no bearing on our freedom and our dignity as an individual in the eyes of God. Therefore, we should not label people with any label that might make them perceive that they are better or worse than other Americans.

Abolish all questions of ethnic heritage and racial background on the census because such questions and answers are demeaning, inaccurate and not worthy of the high standards of our country. The media has an opportunity to state its case and our political leaders have an opportunity to state their case. To me the conclusion is clear; the census should not perpetuate the mistakes of the past. We are all Americans and should be proud to drop all other labels in our pursuit of true tolerance and respect for everyone's human dignity under God.

The teaching of the soul with respect to tolerance is that all human beings are children of God, have a common historical heritage and are related. We are all family. Labels that separate us are not useful in building love and compassion among members of the family of God.

Born Free: Vote to Stay Free

The Declaration of Independence
The Constitution
The Bill of Rights

What a wonderful legacy from previous generations of Americans proud of their country and of their freedom.

To be born in the United States as a citizen or to elect to study and become a naturalized citizen is a great blessing.

At eighteen we are given the privilege to vote to stay free for the rest of our lives in the United States.

We've been through times when voting was limited, but today we don't have to own land or be male to vote.

We can vote: male, female, any ethnic background, any religious background, any racial background, rich or poor, because we are all citizens of the United States.

To be free we must vote. To choose not to vote is to gradually give up our freedom.

Why would anyone voluntarily choose to give up the freedom that we all enjoy and that has been earned for all of us by our ancestors?

We set examples for our children. The only positive example is to vote in every local and national election.

We need to teach our children to cherish our freedom; voting is a perfect way to do so.

Tyranny of our government cannot occur if we all vote.

Tyranny of a vocal minority can occur if we stay home and don't register and vote.

Tyranny is the price we must pay as we gradually lose our freedom by not voting in every election.

Freedom is what we all prefer.

Freedom is our birthright.

Freedom comes and stays with those who are born free and vote to stay free.

Freedom and Responsibility

In the United States, we treasure our freedom: freedom of speech, freedom of the press, freedom to practice the religion of our choice and freedom to select our elected leaders.

Our freedoms do not include the right to steal, murder or commit other crimes. The legal system and the prison system help us to preserve justice for all by punishing those who transgress the laws.

Our soul teaches us to constantly seek positive moral decisions in our lives.

With rights and freedoms, we also have responsibilities. Let's review the responsibilities that our soul teaches:

- Always seek kindness and love over anger and violence.
- Respect and love our fellow human beings.
- If we become parents, take the full responsibility for raising, supporting and training our children.
- Respect the property and rights of others.
- Perform our fair share of the work for our employer.
- Be loyal to our friends and our associates at work.
- Respect and preserve the environment as a legacy for all future generations.

From the power of the freedoms we enjoy also comes our responsibility to use our freedoms to serve God and our fellow human beings.

A Shared Vision

I invite you to share this vision for the citizens of the United States of America and all humans on earth.

We are dedicated to unleashing the tremendous creative potential of all our citizens that has been given to everyone by our Creator.

Our goal is to cherish and protect our U.S. system of freedom, democracy and free enterprise.

We are governed by just laws and we accept the responsibility to abide by those laws as individuals of integrity and morality.

We acknowledge that every human being on earth today has a common heritage and a common Creator of us all. Therefore, we are all family and are expected by our God and Creator to help and serve each other with compassion and love.

We are called to be peacemakers and are dedicated to Peace-of-Mind as

individuals and peace on earth for all
people of our towns, cities, states,
countries and the world.

Our minimum education goal is the completion
of a high quality high school education
by every child and adult in the U.S. We
acknowledge that life-long learning
by all of our citizens is the key to
an excellent standard of living for all.

We respect individual initiative and entrepreneurship.

We acknowledge our need to be responsible
stewards of the land, air, animals, oceans,
lakes and forests.

When difficult financial choices and worldwide
decisions are necessary, the health, safety
and welfare of our citizens of the U.S.
is our first priority.

We vote to protect our freedom.

Reflections On Work

The farmer works hard in his fields and the harvest is good.
The rain and sun from the heavens have blessed
the farmer's work
and the results are satisfying to the farmer, to his family,
to God and to society.
Surely this has been important work, and the farmer has made
a major contribution.
And, in the satisfaction of a job well done,
the farmer is at peace,
and in harmony with this work and the result.
When our work is an important part of our purpose in life,
to love and to be loved, we can truly love our work.
But what if we dislike our work and find
it unsatisfying or even drudgery?
We need only to ask ourselves,
"Is this work helping my soul, my essence,
to grow or to whither?"
If our work is not leading to Peace-of-Mind and a feeling of
satisfaction and contribution, it is our obligation
to ourselves to find other work.
Each person must decide for themselves
what type of work will be a growth mechanism for them.
To work so many hours at unsatisfying work
is not healthy for the growth of the Spirit.
To contribute to the growth of our Spirit, we need work
that is positive and useful to society.

As the Soul Teaches

When we confront an ethics problem.

Ethics in Business

Over the years, I have been involved in many business situations that required ethical decisions. To listen to the teachings of my soul in these situations has been an extremely valuable approach.

Step One: Awareness
   Is there an ethics issue to resolve?
Step Two: Checking Within
   What teaching does your soul offer you on this subject?
Step Three: Decision Making
   What behavior is most appropriate?
Step Four: Reflection
   What are the lessons to remember for the future?

In management positions and in consulting projects, I have uncovered many ethical situations that were instructive.

The following ten examples are ones I have used in teaching situations on the subject of ethics. As you read them, ask yourself the following four questions of each:

   1. Is there an ethics situation to resolve?
   2. What teaching does your soul offer you on this subject?
   3. What behavior is most appropriate?
   4. What are the lessons to remember for the future?

As the Soul Teaches

Business Ethics Cases

1. Chief Executive Officer (CEO) requires Chief Financial Officer (CFO) to report new sales as revenues on the quarterly report to the Securities and Exchange Commission and shareholders. CFO responds that accounting principles are contrary to this practice and that the auditors would not agree. CFO is fired and a new CFO does what the CEO requested. What are the ethics issues?

2. Automobile dealer sells two cars that are exactly alike (the same model, the same color, and so on) for $1,000 less to one customer than the other. Is this just normal negotiations or a matter of an ethics problem?

3. A healthcare provider licensed software and agreed in the business contract to not compete with the software supplier during the term of the agreement and for two years after the end of the agreement. The software supplier also agreed not to compete with the healthcare provider. The healthcare provider then purchased a competitive software supplier. Beyond the legal issues, what are the business ethics issues?

4. A sales representative closed a $100,000 contract and received a $25,000 commission. In order to complete the contract, extensive assistance was provided by the home office staff. The home office staff received no extra compensation but did receive a personal thank you note from the salesperson. What management structures are involved, and what are

the potential business ethics issues?

5. A sales representative exceeds her sales goal by 80%. She receives her appropriate commissions and bonus. Her territory for the next year is cut in half. She hears through the grapevine that the reason for the territory change is that she made more total dollars for the year than her manager. What are the ethics issues in this situation?

6. Two candidates for employment appear to be almost equally qualified for the position. The corporation has set a goal to hire more women and minorities. The person who receives the job did not receive the best reports from the interviewers and was asking for more starting salary than the other candidates. What are the business ethics issues?

7. A U.S. plastics supplier is seeking to obtain business in Italy. The company's sales representative in Italy says they can get the $100,000 contract if the company pays a $15,000 fee to the nephew of the buyer for being a distributor in Italy. What are the ethical issues?

8. A Japanese healthcare products distributor signs a three-year agreement to distribute a U.S. manufacturer's product. At the end of the three years, the U.S. manufacturer is surprised to find that the distributor has converted all of its clients to an almost identical product supplied by a Japanese manufacturer. Is there an ethics problem?

9. A large corporation offers to acquire a small corporation as soon as appropriate "due diligence" studies are completed (analyzing the small company's products, services, staff, suppliers, agreements with clients and all financial records over the past three years, and so on). After two-thirds of the due diligence studies are completed, the large company decides not to proceed with the acquisition. Within six months, the large company is competing with the small company with its own product and service offerings. What business ethics issues are involved in this situation?

10. A trade association endorses the product of one of the suppliers to the members of the association. There are 100 suppliers of a similar product. The supplier chosen is a major advertiser in the journal of the association and has promised major discounts to the association members. The product has been tested and sent back for further development six times over the past two years and has no commercial users. What are the business ethics questions?

In each of the scenarios, did you find yourself pondering the question, "I wonder what is legal in this situation?"

The legal issues are, of course, important. For this exercise, however, I recommend that you concentrate on the ethics issues by listening to the teachings of your soul. By asking the four questions on each situation, you will have internalized the process of wrestling ethics issues in business. After repetition of the four questions on the ten situations, you will have experienced a new way of reflecting on ethics situations.

Here is another perspective on ethics issues. Answer the following question for yourself before you make a decision, "Is this decision questionable or would I be completely comfortable if the situation were reported on the front page of the local newspaper?" The teachings of your soul and the "front page of the local newspaper" question, will together guide you to ethical decisions.

About Work and Society

"We, the people of the United States...derived from the consent of the governed."

A major new concept of government was launched with these words. The "consent of the governed" gave power to all citizens. It took a while to provide the right to vote to slaves as citizens, not possessions. It took a while to provide the right to vote to women also. But, over time, the model of government was refined to include all citizens. The original concept was powerful and the people accepted it as proper so it has been the basis for the healthy growth of our method of government.

Consider the evolution of society and business.

In Stone Age times and beyond, the family unit joined others to form tribes. Tribal leaders prevailed around the world. Monarchies, emperors and such were a step that divided societies into the very rich, the very poor and a small middle class. As kings were overturned, societies still had economic strata but the middle class grew in size. The democratic principles made it possible for one generation of a family to improve themselves economically from the previous generation. The broadened availability of education opportunities was very important in this evolution.

The concept of representative government where power is derived from the consent of the governed would seem strange to the builders of the pyramids with their slave labor.

The thoughts of economic and social fairness have evolved greatly over the centuries, but of course are not uniformly applied around the world.

The view of society with a long-term perspective can be very interesting. Changes seem small from day to day, but over the centuries the changes in society are very large.

The battle of democracy versus communism captured much of our attention in the twentieth century. We now talk about a global economy and global communication easily and they are only possible because of the peaceful solution to differences. Wars became more and more severe throughout history as weapons became more powerful, and now economic solutions have mostly replaced the usefulness of war to improve the standard of living of the people in a country.

Will we be free of wars led by power-hungry leaders? No, but gradually other solutions are becoming more attractive. The model of freedom, democracy and the free enterprise system is attractive to more and more people around the world.

The teachings of the soul throughout history are consistent: practice unconditional love to your fellow humans as God has loved all humans. We learn from the soul, our divine internal observer, to be kind, loving and compassionate to all the members of our human family.

As the Soul Teaches

Life in Perspective

Peace-of-Mind is ours when we listen to the teachings of our soul. In our life from womb to eternity, our soul provides direction to the paths to the most joyous and rewarding of life's experiences—love and close personal relationships.

Thinking About Thinking

From my personal experiences, I suggest that human beings exist and think on ten different levels of consciousness. The soul is advising the thinking of the brain at every level.

Recall a conversation when you were about to tell someone about another person and couldn't recall her name. You finally gave up trying to remember the name, walked to another part of your home to check the status of the wash in the washing machine, and the name flashed to your consciousness—Shirley Larson. Where did the name come from, suddenly, when you were focusing on the washing? Most likely, part of your brain was working on the search for the name in your memory bank while another part of your brain was focusing on the washing.

Dreams clearly come from another part of our brain than our normal conscious communications. Dreams, along with prayer, meditation, and our life experiences are routes to determine God's will for us.

Some people have fears of heights, elevators or thunder. These fears, psychologists tell us, were learned by our brains at a very young age—usually by age five. Of course, through our life experiences, we can program our brain to give us feedback. We don't like the taste of peas until adulthood, or maybe never. When we see peas our brain sends out a "yuk" signal and we don't want to even see peas, let alone eat them.

Addictions are a message from our brain that we enjoy a certain experience (chocolate, coffee, cigarettes, and so on).

Our conscious mind might decide to avoid chocolate, but when it is available, another portion of our brain—the subconscious or unconscious—sends the message that we act on. And we eat the chocolate.

Fears and addictions influence us as if they are programmed into our brains. But, wonder of wonders, our brain can be reprogrammed, if we choose to do so. After all, it is our brain. We can program chocolate as "yuk" and peas as "yummy," if we choose to do so.

However, as we all know, reprogramming the brain is not easy, but it can be done. Reprogramming based on the soul's teachings will enrich our life.

When the brain has many fears, anxieties and angers that we choose to change, we have to work at it. Psychiatrists and psychologists make their living by listening to and counseling people on the messages from their brains. This little chapter isn't intended to cover the depth of Freud, Jung and medical experts but only to explore briefly our multiple levels of consciousness.

Here is a list of ten levels of consciousness that I have experienced and, I suspect on reflection, most humans have experienced. The reason this list is of interest to me is that it has proven to be so valuable. On many occasions I have assigned a problem to my subconscious or unconscious and been delighted to find that the problem and solution are presented to my conscious mind days or weeks later. It is a thrill every time this occurs, and those thrilling thinking experiences have now occurred thousands of times in my life.

Ten Potential Levels of Consciousness

1. Nonverbal communication person-to-person (for example, wink of the eye, tilt of the head, smile).
2. Normal person-to-person conversation.
3. Prayer/meditation.
4. Daydreaming/reverie.
5. Slightly awake from a dream; know it's a dream, but want to continue.
6. Dreams while you are asleep related to the activities of your day.
7. Observing yourself in a dream, as an outside observer from a distance.
8. Ability to influence the course of a dream during the dream.
9. Unexplained view of the future.
10. Conversation with a divine force within you.

In my experience, conscious thought occurs in levels 1, 2, 3 and 4. Subconscious thought occurs in levels 3, 4, 5 and 6. Unconscious thought occurs in levels 5, 6, 7, 8, 9, and 10. What is your experience?

If we listen to our soul and choose love and trust and program them into our brains, we see love and trust in the world. If we program in fear, anger and deceit, we see fear, anger and deceit in the world. Who suffers from anger? We do. When we are angry, our body and soul feel the physical and emotional effects. Yet how many people are angry with others who they haven't even seen for five years or who are

As the Soul Teaches

dead? Only the person who has the anger suffers. So why keep the anger? Do we want to victimize ourselves? Yes, many people do. I choose not to be a victim.

To program forgiveness to replace anger in our thinking is very difficult but very positive for our mental health and Peace-of-Mind.

Messages from our soul are always flowing toward us, perhaps in ten or more different levels of consciousness.

Time

Yesterday, today, tomorrow and eternity—that's all there is.

Up until now, the days have been our yesterdays. They are our yesterdays, whether they have been sad or glad, full of love or full of anger and hate, full of joy or anxiety, full of birth or death, full of new experiences or repeating the old. Our mind and memories are filled with the experiences of our yesterdays. Our thoughts and memories tap into our yesterdays and remind us of the way things were.

But we only live in today. Tomorrow and eternity lie before us as we live each day as today. A rich tomorrow is our today when we wake up each morning. Our life begins in our mother's womb and is shaped in every yesterday, today and tomorrow.

If we set Peace-of-Mind for eternity as our goal in peace and love, our soul will guide us toward that goal.

As the sands move through the hourglass, time moves from now to a new now. Today and now is where we live on earth. But with an eye on eternity, our soul guides us as each grain of sand passes through the hourglass of our life.

We know there is a time to live. It is now. Do not wait! There is a time for compassion. It is now. Do not wait! There is a time to communicate your love and caring for others. It is now. Do not wait! There is a time for forgiving ourselves and forgiving others. It is now. Do not wait!

Hate, anger, violence—these are the baser side of our beings that we must strive to let our soul chase from the now and let only love, compassion and forgiveness envelop us. Our Creator has given us free will but wishes that we would listen to the positive teachings of our souls.

Time and love are all we truly have to give to another. To spend time with another is our greatest gift. Time is ours to spend wisely so that our soul can soar and our lives can be enriched as we enrich the lives of others.

We Are Our Perception of Ourselves

As a human being, the Creator has made each of us unique individuals with incredible potential for good.

If our perception of our uniqueness is positive as we learn from our soul, then we will lead a positive, enthusiastic life. Our positive perception of ourselves and our unlimited potential for joy, hope and love help us build our character.

We are our perception of ourselves.

Suppose we lie to the people with whom we associate. Suppose we behave against the guidance of our soul but seek the approval of others, so we lie to provide others with false information that will cause them to think highly of us. Such action creates a great tension between the teachings of our soul and our verbal pronouncements that are lies compared to our actual behavior.

We can lie to others to try to hide the real truth. When we do, those lies may have a temporary benefit to our image in the world. But when the real truth becomes known, our image suffers badly because we have been caught in a lie—a cover-up of our true behavior.

Our real approval in life comes from being unconditionally accepted and loved by our Creator and our soul. We don't need the approval of others, so we don't need to lie.

Let's consider a practical example:

A child cheats at school by copying someone else's homework because he hasn't done his assignment. The lie is to his teacher, his classmates, his parents and himself. The teaching of the soul has been ignored. When the truth of his behavior is uncovered, he is in much more trouble with his teacher, his classmates and his parents than if he had admitted up front that he didn't do his homework. The truth may hurt, but a lot less than a lie that is uncovered.

So the child concludes, "Don't get caught. If you aren't caught, you win. You have duped the teacher, your classmates and your parents." But if you aren't caught cheating, you have still cheated and your soul knows it. Therefore, you have burdened your soul with a fake image in the outside world versus the truth of your cheating. That's what mental health problems are made of—anxiety and depression from lies.

Why do people lie? Much of the influence to lie probably comes from our youth. If our parents expect high standards of behavior but accept a shortcoming or mistake lovingly and with forgiveness, we are more encouraged to tell the truth than cover up with a lie. Our parents love us unconditionally, in this case, and disapprove of our bad behavior, but they still love us and show us that love.

When parents are extremely harsh with punishments, they are trying to help their child using the element of fear. The mechanism of fear can lead children to lie so they don't have to pay the consequences of their behavior—at least not immediately. With an atmosphere a fear generated by parents, lying seems like a protection mechanism. When parents use love rather than fear, the need to lie vanishes.

As we grow up and mature, our mind and soul still remember the lessons of our youth. We can reparent ourselves, but it takes a lot of effort.

What is your perception of yourself? Are you proud of

telling the truth, or have you lied often to seek approval of others?

To lie is to gradually tear down the goodness of our essence, to damage our character and to dismiss the potential for joy, hope and unconditional love in our life.

Forgiveness

Forgiveness is about relationships.
Forgiveness is the key to the
success of relationships.
We know that our Creator, God, will
forgive us, because God is the
essence of unconditional love.
We must have the willingness to accept
God's forgiveness, and also
forgive ourselves for falling short
of what we know is right, true,
and in the spirit of unconditional love in
our relationships.
But how are we to forgive others?
First, we must value the person we are
about to forgive as a child of God,
just like ourselves.
If God loves me and God
loves the other person, it is a
reasonable commitment for
me to love that person.
Forgiveness is then a natural step of
extending unconditional love to others as
God does to us.
Some say we should forgive and forget.
To forgive is to say that we will not
hold the past as our dominant
memory for the future.

We can forgive without completely forgetting the
situation that required forgiveness.
Forgiveness has a value to both
parties of the relationship. Often
mutual forgiveness is very useful.
Forgiveness is a critical part of
every lasting relationship. I
am convinced that God planned it that way.
We have free will from our Creator
and therefore, we must make the conscious choice
to forgive others or not.
The teachings of our soul are consistent
with God's unconditional love.

The Power of the Hug

A hug from another human being is
- as glorious as a beautiful sunrise,
- as nurturing as our mother's touch,
- as spectacular as a Chopin concerto,
- as exhilarating as winning a race,
- as gentle as a kiss,
- as emotional as being in love,
- as satisfying as being recognized,
- as comforting as a baby in the womb, and
- as exciting as our best dreams.

It takes two to hug. One person must offer, usually by opening his or her arms-one high and one low. The other person can respond with a similar extension of arms or not choose to hug by not extending arms. It's a choice.

How wonderful it is when friends feel comfortable greeting each other with a hug. It is a sign of openness and love. It takes some courage to initiate a hug because it might not be acknowledged. But when it is, both parties have connected in a meaningful way.

Different societies view such physical contact of two human beings with acceptance or alarm.

As humans, we all crave the physical touch of those we love. To be held in the embrace of a hug is a measure of tender affection.

A hug is powerful because it is a form of physical bonding in the atmosphere of kindness, gentleness and unconditional love.

Mother and child understand a hug. Perhaps everyone should remember the child within them that wants to give and receive hugs.

Our soul is nurtured when we experience a positive relationship with another human being. The power of the hug is in its response to the teachings of our soul as we seek Peace-of-Mind.

A Successful Life

Is it possible to measure success?
Is it measured in possessions or dollars?
Is the most successful person
in life the one who dies with
the most material wealth?

Or is success measured in love?
Is the person who loves unconditionally
throughout his or her life the most successful?
At the end of life on earth,
how do we measure the love
that a person spread to others?

Let us consult with our soul.
To love and to be loved, that is
the essence of a successful life.
Our spiritual existence started in our
mother's womb and continues to eternity.
Our materialistic life starts at our
birth and ends at our physical death.
Success is better measured in love
than in material possessions.
We learn that principle when we
listen attentively to the teachings of our soul.

We Make the Choices

God gave us free will and a soul to teach us, then we make the choices.

With the gift of free will comes the responsibility for accepting the results of our choices.

As children, our choices are strongly controlled by our parents, but as we grow and mature, our choices become our responsibility.

- We choose between kindness to others or abuse of others.
- We choose between love or hate.
- We choose between compassion or violence.
- We choose between smoking or not smoking.
- We choose between chemical substance abuse or refraining from drug and alcohol use.
- We choose between tolerance of the rights of other humans or intolerance.
- We choose to work hard or to avoid work.
- We choose to work hard at school to learn all we can or to skip classes and not study.
- We choose to obey the laws or violate them.
- We choose to vote or not vote.
- We choose to help build our community or destroy our community.
- We choose to associate with groups who are promoting peace or those who are promoting violence.
- We choose to support our family or abandon them.

- We choose to listen to the teachings of our soul or to ignore them.
- We choose our friends, our acquaintances and our spouses.
- We make the choices; who among us could believe otherwise?

Life is made up of thousands of choices; our choices will match the hope that God has for us if we follow the positive and enriching teachings of our soul.

Ignore the teachings of our soul and we must take the full responsibility for the consequences in our life. That's free will from God.

Peace-of-Mind

Tranquil and not anxious.
Confident and not apprehensive.
Courageous and not fearful.

Peace is a state of mind, a comfort for the soul.

Peace is always in the presence of God.

We are at peace in our mother's womb and at peace in heaven for eternity.

Eternal peace is always ours as God's gift.

What a wondrous gift our mind is.

The minds of all of God's children are capable of peace.

But what of suffering? Why do some humans have tortured souls and absence of peace?

It is not ours to know all the mysteries of the universe.

But this we do know: God's will for us is that our soul and our mind should be at peace, peace within and peace with all other human beings.

Where there is anger, we substitute love.

Where there is hurt, we offer compassion.

Where there is hate, we offer tolerance.

We reap what we sow; let us sow love, compassion and tolerance,

And we have Peace-of-Mind and a joyful soul.

Appendix

About the Author

Bill Peter is a management consultant, philosopher, realtor and author who lives in a suburb of Minneapolis, Minnesota. By prayer, personal experiences, meditation and dreams, he has learned his personal mission in life:

- To love and be loved,
- to seek Peace-of-Mind always,
- to grow personally in spirit and contributions to society,
- to live by principles that set a good example, and
- to help others grow by being available as a coach.

This book is Book Three in the "Peace-of-Mind" Series by Bill Peter. Book Four is planned for publication in 2000.

For additional information about Bill Peter as a speaker, author, and management consultant, please visit: www.billpeter.com.

As the Soul Teaches

Order Form for *As the Soul Teaches*

TO: Bill Peter & Associates
       6650 Vernon Hills Road, Edina, MN 55436

Your name:_____
Your address:_____
           _____
           _____

Home Phone:_____Work Phone:_____

Please mail your order to the address above along with your personal check.
Signature: _____
Order Date: _____

Copies of *As the Soul Teaches* at $6.00 per copy   = $_____
(60% discount from $14.95 price - minimum order
of 24 copies)

Shipping and Handling: (Allow 2 weeks for delivery -
$10.00 per case of 24 copies)   = $_____

Total Cost (Your Personal Check Enclosed)   = $_____

(For larger orders, call toll-free 1-877-466-6846 for a price quote.)

For information - Call toll-free: 1-877-466-6846

"Peace-of-Mind" Series by Bill Peter

Book Three:
"Peace-of-Mind" (our moral behavior).
As the Soul Teaches.

Book Two:
"Peace-of-Mind" (our work).
Unleashing Business Creativity…to empower your clients.

Book One:
"Peace-of-Mind" (our home).
"I'M MOVING" **- Eliminating the anxiety of buying or selling a home.**

As the Soul Teaches

© 2000 by Bill Peter.

No part of this book may be reproduced by any mechanical, photographic or electronic process, or in the form of an audio recording, nor may it be stored in a retrieval system, transmitted, or otherwise copied for public or private use without written permission from the author and publisher.

All rights reserved.

Printed in the United States of America.

Library of Congress Catalog Card Number: 00 190527

ISBN 1-890676-60-8

Beaver's Pond Press
Edina, Minnesota